Common Sense Purchasing

Visit www.commonsensepurchasing.com to order the book

Common Sense Purchasing

Hard Knock Lessons Learned From a
Purchasing Pro

Dr. Tom DePaoli

2004

Common Sense Purchasing

Introduction

This book is a compilation of my experiences in purchasing and the tough lessons that I have learned over the years. It includes some of my articles and lessons learned from the struggles of my extensive reengineering of purchasing. I have repeated some important points throughout the book and tried to keep the lessons of common sense purchasing short and poignant. My personal journey in purchasing has been a creative adventure. However, like most good things in life it has had its disappointments. I have learned much more from my failures than my successes and feel much stronger because of them. It has been fun in a strange and spectacular way! I have learned much from the adventure and from my personal colleagues and friends. I can't thank them enough for their support. I admit that I have made just about every darn mistake that one can make in purchasing. The key is that I have corrected them and hopefully become wiser and smarter because of them. I have held every purchasing position from junior buyer to vice president. They have given me a unique view of people, organizations and systems. Like purchasing itself, some of this book is just boring like homework and is merely a checklist to help you. The majority are the key common sense techniques you will need to succeed. The important stuff I have repeated because common sense is all too uncommon and takes lots of practice.

My great thanks to Darren Johnson my very creative illustrator.

Enjoy the purchasing journey and keep exploring.

Visit my website at www.commonsenspurchasing.com

This book is dedicated to my family, my wife Terry, my sons Tommy and Joey and my daughter Roseanne. They have all supported me throughout my journey in life and I love them dearly. My parents Martin and Anne also played such a strong role in molding my character and instilling the importance of integrity and respect for others that when I started purchasing I already had these two most important skills for success. My parents always put their children first ahead of themselves. When I had a tough decision to make in purchasing, I just asked myself what would my Mom and Dad do and I was always right. To them I owe a heck of a lot. I can't fail to mention my brothers and sisters Ed, Tony, Carol and Rosemary. They put up with me when I was growing up and made sure I got away with more than most children do. They were good alibi witnesses for me. Of course their motive was that if I got away with it; that would just make it easier for them to get away with something even more preposterous. They were just fun to grow up with and very smart, almost as smart as me. My mother came from a family of seven siblings and my father from a family of fifteen. I must mention all my aunts and uncles who played a key role in influencing me. As a kid I was co-raised in the fifties and sixties in a small town literally by an Army of Italian aunts and uncles who not only cared dearly for me but kept me out of trouble, which for a child as rambunctious, too smart for his own good, and rebellious as me was no small task. Special thanks to Uncle Mario and Aunt Lucy my godparents, Uncle Pat and Aunt Peggy, Aunt Alberta and

Uncle Joe, Aunt Anna Marie, Aunt Gloria, Uncle Arley, Uncles Don and Frank and my adopted Uncle Ollie. All my grandparents were wonderful and my son bears the middle name of Grand Pop Liberatore who entertained me perpetually with stories, Bible quotes, and jokes. I could not have had better relatives and cousins to share my upbringing. They have blessed my life. For more information on my upbringing read my book Growing Up Italian in the 50s. It is available on Amazon.com and visit my website www.growingupmemories.com. Although I have four university degrees I must thank the United States Military with whom I have been associated with now for five decades now. They taught me true leadership and how to lead by example. More importantly they made sure that I double checked all that so called academic theoretical stuff they teach us in school. Ninety five percent of it doesn't work. They taught me how to recognize the five percent that does. They also taught me that honor, courage and commitment are ideals that you must live and abide by with others at all times.Enjoy the book!

1. It's About Relationships First And Foremost.

Purchasing is the art of building relationships. It is not about negotiations, transactions, industry knowledge, market knowledge, know-how or technology. It is all about building strong relationships and gaining the trust of suppliers, customers, and colleagues. Nothing else comes close to building relationships in importance for successful purchasing. A purchasing professional must be able to build relationships or they are about as useless as a screen door on a submarine. They may need to pursue another career. Do not spend inordinate amounts of money on so called purchasing technical training unless a strong foundation of relationships is well underway. You cannot fake relationships. You cannot legislate it. Purchasing professionals need to live it and commit to it. Integrity in relationships will always carry the day, impress suppliers, scare the competition, and let you sleep well at night. Educational credentials look good, and certifications are impressive but nothing makes a purchasing professional more effective than developing strong relationships and being true to their word. Spending more time on relationships almost always pays off for all participants. Once trust or relationships are broken they are nearly impossible to repair, so do not neglect them or underestimate their criticality. You will not be able to dig yourself out of any of the deep holes that you dig by dishonest relationships. Smoozing is a lot easier than shoveling. Honesty builds respect.

2. How Do You Build Relationships?

The best way to build relationships is to do what you say you are going to do, always follow through on your words with actions, and to hold yourself accountable for your actions. Working together problem solving with the suppliers you are trying to build a relationship with is always a strong way to enhance relationships. Nothing beats sympathy and genuine caring about their struggles and personal fears. People remember when you take the time to personally help them through difficult times or issues. During a crisis if you can help a person solve an urgent problem or issue by going the extra mile you will get their gratitude and trust. Treating others like you want to be treated is the surest way to build relationships. The golden rule works. Use it.

3. Plan or Perish. Make Sure You Have a Strategy First Not Technology First.

Institute for Supply Management notes that 95% of procurement organizations do not have a procurement strategy or long-term plan. Of the 5% that do have a strategy, only half have successfully aligned the strategy with overall business strategy. Most purchasing departments are continually embroiled in tactics and mountains of transactions. Much of their energy is distracted to the intensive transactions for (80% of the work) low dollar volume (20% of the dollars) aspects of the supply chain. A procurement or supply chain strategy must be in place and visible. Ideally it should be the linchpin of the corporate strategy and lead the company. Do not ever attempt any transformation or change in purchasing without a sound strategy and upper management buy in. You will perish. It's not a pleasant death.

4. Sign up a Champion Not a Chump.

If you want to play like a champion you have got to have one on your side. This needs to be a person with strong leadership ability, clout and respect in the organization. Too often inappropriate or weak champions (chumps or tomato cans) are appointed to transform purchasing. The champion needs to have a siege mentality and perseverance. Resistance to changes in procurement is especially fierce. It is a cultural battleground that needs a general to make bold and tough decisions. A take no prisoners' mentality certainly helps. The champion must not be afraid to discipline those who do not change or who violate governance rules. This discipline is necessary for success. Many folks cannot deal with discipline. Do not put them in leadership positions.

5. Why the Siege Mentality?

Often in companies and in the purchasing traditional culture supplier relationships have existed for years. The good old boys are really good old boys and have cemented their networks. Maverick buying, breaking the rules and awkward supplier relationships are the norm. Relationships are strong but based on the whims or needs of purchasing folks or other internal customers. Suppliers love a divided corporate house. It is much easier to confuse than impress. Bottom line a coordinated team approach to relationships is necessary. A disciplined strategy that meets the total needs of a corporation and not just a few departments is alien to most companies. You need a siege mentality, perseverance, and always being prepared for a long tedious battle. Be prepared for constantly being challenged and subject to all types of tricks to derail the strategy. You will either become a survivalist or you will remain a victim. The former is healthier.

6. Ruthlessly Rationalize Suppliers First and Don't Back Off.

Radically reducing the number of suppliers is one of the first efforts that must be tackled. You cannot have "relationships" with thousands of suppliers. It is difficult enough to have strong relationships with just a few key suppliers. Ruthlessness is necessary. This is not the time for compassion or backing off your supplier reduction goals. Set the new supplier standards high. You will be surprised. Many will not want to participate under your new higher expectations. Does the supplier actually add value or is the supplier a product of misplaced loyalty? I once cut a base of 5000 suppliers to 252 in three months. It can be done but ruthlessness is required.

Purchasing departments have been implementing supply base rationalization strategies since the latter half of the 1990s in order to reduce the administrative costs associated with a large number of suppliers, to streamline purchasing processes, and to improve control over inventory. In purchasing and supply departments, supplier consolidation or supply base rationalization continues. It is understood to mean identifying the ideal number of suppliers, often reducing the current amount. The trend toward supplier rationalization has continued dramatically even as purchasing and supply managers have begun to contend with the possibilities and challenges presented by the rise of e-procurement, which at first glance may seems incompatible with rationalization. After all, with extensive search capabilities available through any Web browser, and with the proliferation of electronic storefronts and virtual markets, e-procurement promises to open up a world of potential new suppliers that can be identified through the Internet.

E-procurement supports supply base reduction so long as the focus remains on rationalization as a strategy and on e-procurement as a tool to facilitate that strategy. The implication is that growth in the virtual marketplace could be working to increase some organizations' supply bases. Purchasing and supply managers at several organizations currently implementing e-procurement systems assert that these systems will in fact support their ongoing supply base rationalization strategies. Do not procrastinate. Get on with it. Slash your suppliers as soon as possible. Do not back off.

7. Know Your Suppliers and Know Their Industry.

The very best piece of negotiations advice I ever received was to know the capabilities of your supplier, their industry, their competitors, their cost drivers, their margins and their capabilities better than they do! This is extremely difficult but it is a powerful tool. It requires a lot of homework, digging and flat out work. Once a supplier realizes you understand them, it eliminates all the negotiation game playing and posturing. You will be surprised how fast they can now focus on real issues and problem solving once they know you can't be bamboozled. You obviously cannot do this with every supplier only the most important and most strategic ones. It is a powerful negotiation tactic based on knowledge not histrionics. Level the playing field with your knowledge! Roll up your sleeves, dig deep and become an industry expert. Suppliers will be impressed with your knowledge.

8. Which Suppliers to Partner With and How Many.

Do not generate a plethora of partnerships of alliances with suppliers. True partnerships are deep relationships, and they must be tightly controlled and evaluated. It makes no sense to partner with hundreds of suppliers just for the sake of using the partnership term. True partnerships require a great deal of energy, relationship effort and time.

One of the prime criteria's to select a supplier as a partner is the fact that they have had previous partner experience. This is a tremendous advantage and should not be discounted at all in your criteria. Think of partnering as important as a long term marriage and treat it as such. Divorces are bloody so choose carefully the supplier partner.

9. Sizing up Your Suppliers and Preparing Them for Your Strategy.

Suppliers that have had experience with non-traditional purchasing concepts, alliances and partnerships have an advantage when it comes to developing a deep relationship with them. Make sure you take the time to explain your procurement or supply chain strategy to them and to take the time to understand their strategy. They need to know what's in it for them. Make it clear and measurable. Feeling good about each other doesn't get to the bottom line. Appearances do count. You can size up a supplier's partner quotient by actual site visits and talking to their employees at all levels. Smiling faces are better than growls and disgruntled remarks. This new frontier with suppliers has some particular characteristics. These characteristics include most favored customer contracts, elimination of incoming inspection, reduction of supplier base, early supplier involvement in design, value engineering, mutual cost reductions, targeting of non-production company costs, the complete integration of key suppliers into the business, and extensive use of cross-functional teams.

This quantum leap philosophy with suppliers requires the education of purchasing personnel, rapid access to information and supplier empowerment. Cross-functional business teams and a constant dedication to improve and to reduce time to market are key elements.

10. Retraining Procurement Professionals. Bids Protect No One.

Unfortunately many procurement professionals do not want to learn new approaches or non traditional purchasing. The key is to train them to relate to suppliers, customers, etc. No matter what you try if they do not believe in the process in their heart or gut they will not change. It is hard to teach trust, integrity or character. These above all else are necessary for procurement professionals. Traditional purchasing rewards the exact wrong skills and behaviors. It rewards pencil pushers and mindless bureaucrats. Requirements are basically dictated or thrown over the wall to purchasing who often select a supplier by a rigid bid process. Ironically most non-purchasing employees think the bid process somehow protects a company. Purchasing professionals soon realize the exact opposite is true. It is a process beret with danger and dishonesty. Price is often king. Cheap is regarded as better. The buying department is often heavily transaction focused with multiple and complicated steps just to purchase an item no matter how small or cheap. Requisitions drive the workload and the rules inhibit any real relationships with suppliers. Customer needs go out the window and procedures, bids and contracts rule.

Progressive purchasing is highly team focused especially cross-functional teams. The examination of the supply chain and total cost of ownership drives the decision making process. There is a systematic process for supplier selection. Relationship building and management is the key skill for the purchasing professional. When senior management not only supports but also understands the process, purchasing becomes a true business partner and leader.

11. Hammers Are For Nails. Match Tools To The Materials And Services.

Try to match the procurement tool to the material and more importantly to the internal customer trying to use the tool. For routine MRO items speed, ease of use and a no hassle approach are the key components. The person buying a routine consumable item does not want to be bogged down with offensive audits, logs, etc. They want to buy the darn item or part and get it delivered quickly. Always remember that electronic purchasing of a routine item is competing with the easiest way to buy it. Pick up a phone speed dial the supplier and order the part and hang up. This is quick and easy and more importantly painless to the end-user. Do not give them even more pain with a so called better systems or superficial checks and balances.

12. Doing Your Homework with Suppliers and Industries.

Make sure you dig up the standard industry references about industries and do your homework on which suppliers or companies are at the top in the industry. In most industries there are 3 or 4 top companies and although there are differences on many routine items or commodities you can't go very wrong by picking one of the top 3 or 4 as your supplier. Don't over procrastinate on these types of items. Top management needs to understand one important precept. Suppliers can make or break any business or business plan. According to Dr. Deming defective materials or equipment not human error or the defective process causes over 80% of quality variances. Suppliers obviously play the key role in achieving high quality. Suppliers need to be treated as stakeholders not adversaries. World-class suppliers can become a company's very best competitive weapons. They play the quintessence role in reducing time to market.

The major challenges of the next century include maximizing supplier contributions by focusing on supplier partners and on continuous improvement. The focus must be on quality, flexibility and reducing time to market. Ultimately company performance is judged by the paying customers or what I call the final end-user customer. Typically purchasing gets totally sidetracked and thinks that internal company customers are their real customers. Nothing could be further from the truth. These internal customers often whipsaw purchasing into doing stupid human tricks to satisfy their exaggerated needs. Purchasing is not an unctuous service organization at the beck and whim of internal customers. It is the chief revenue center for the corporation. It should in conjunction with sales find out exactly what the paying customers want not boisterous internal customers. Internal customers often just confuse the true end customer needs issue. Purchasing when in the reengineering process needs to focus on what specification the ultimate paying customer wants not the false specifications of engineering, manufacturing, shipping accounting, etc. Examine if their needs add value. This is a heck of a lot easier said than done. This is one reason why companies spend millions on customer research and focus groups. Many internal departments think they are the chief customers. Worse, they all think they know what the final customer wants. They are usually dead wrong.

An initial internal customers' needs assessment checklist should include things like what are people's expectations from purchasing. Don't expect any major insights here. Often their expectations are mired in traditional thinking and self-serving tunnel vision requirements. Purchasing needs to understand what they are evaluated on and how the score is kept. Price reductions are often only five to ten percent of the savings potential for a company. New reporting relationships must be discussed. A new organization must be proposed and agreed upon in advance. Purchasing needs to get more involved in the design phase of products and coexist with sales in order to get to know the paying customer up front and personal and then challenge what the customer really needs. A customer resource assessment is required. This is not a process that can be done part time. Unless people and the team are completely dedicated to the process it will fail. Resistance to change will be fierce and harsh. One way to overcome the resistance is to insure that communications of changes are open and outstanding. It is important to wisely choose a very first project or reengineering task. Initial success in this project is critical for future success. Success does snowball. Often it is wise to pick the process that is the rift with redundancy and a clear easy victory when basic streamlining is accomplished. The reengineering team must be trained in the process and a facilitator is highly recommended. The team needs to prepare to be under siege and be aware of the rule of change. In order to effect a change in most organizations you must adhere to the seven times rule. A change must be presented and driven for at least seven times and explained seven different ways in order for it to start to take hold in an organization.

13. Doing an Assessment of Where You Spend Your Money.

You need to know where you are spending your money. If you don't the process is doomed to failure. Here are some questions to ask:
• What are your major categories of purchases?

- Are you currently using EDI or other electronic means for purchasing payment or processes?
- Do you receive summary billing from some suppliers?
- Do you use blanket orders? List them and their annual value.
- Do you have a stores system that is online and linked to purchasing?
- Does your account payable system link other site systems?
- Do you releases for some buying?
- How many types of forms of techniques do you use to purchase? List them.
- How many people work in purchasing and accounts payable?
- Do you use corporate purchase cards?
- How many purchasing transactions in a week—month—year?
- What is your dollar volume of purchases in the same above time frames?
- Can you list alphabetically suppliers with the following data?
- Can you list stores or stockroom suppliers with the same above data?
- Do you have any special terms or conditions with suppliers? List them.
- What percent of purchase discounts do you capture?
- What are your average days to pay a supplier?
- What is the average dollar value of your purchase orders? How many under $1000?
- Approximately how many people purchase goods or materials? How many over 25 times a year?
- Would you say that your purchases are centralized or decentralized and why?

In a typical company, 75% of all invoices are for purchases of under $1,000. At an average cost of $100 to $250 or more to process the purchase order, pay the invoice, and handle all the related paperwork, this represents a tremendous overhead cost for most businesses. Indeed, in many cases the cost of handling the paperwork can be greater than the value of the actual items that were purchased. In this area, e-procurement solutions are relatively well developed. Ariba, Oracle, IBM and many other providers offer e-commerce applications that streamline and automate the entire workflow from issuing purchase orders, getting documents approved, paying invoices, and updating appropriate budget and financial systems. These approaches typically result in dropping the cost of fully processing transactions down to perhaps $25, some as low as $3 per transaction — a reduction of as much as 90%. In addition the typical analysis reveals that purchasing *spends at least 50% or more of their time just on acquisitions!* Do not let the bureaucracy bog down purchasing.

14. Smashing Traditional Procurement Culture. Change Everything. Change it!

The traditional procurement environment dies hard. My advice is to change everything. Job title, roles, nomenclature even work area change helps. If you are dedicated to cross functional teams a true purchasing professional will be out of the purchasing area most of the time. Do not let purchasing folks regress to old habits. It takes a person at least thirty days to gain a new habit. Get everyone completely out of their comfort zone and starting to do the tough work of relationship building.

15. Testing Suppliers Capabilities. Always Do A Road Test.

Never incorporate a new supplier without an actual test run of buying an item from them period and no exceptions. Have a purchasing professional "pretend" they are an end user, play dumb and actually order an item form the new supplier. Review the entire transaction process to include acknowledgement and invoice payment. Check on status often. This one road test tip will save you mountains of headaches and resistance to change. Folks do not really want new suppliers. They will latch on to any mistake to justify their resistance and castigate the new supplier.

16. Get A Comprehensive Sourcing Methodology. Get One. Clone One. Stick To It.

There are many comprehensive sourcing or supplier selection models available. Most require careful research and a team approach. Remember these are meant for important suppliers, materials or services or the ones that have a big impact on the bottom line. Do not waste time on such a thorough process for the little fish or routine purchases. Strategic sourcing is a disciplined process organizations implement in order to more efficiently purchase goods and services from suppliers. The goal is to reduce total acquisition cost while improving value. Forrester reports that 40% of the total reductions in costs are associated with technology while the other 60% are associated with strategic sourcing techniques. Here are my four key points to jump start strategic sourcing:

- Understand the state of current spending.
- Prepare a sourcing strategy for particular commodities and tie the strategy into business and e-business strategy.
- Evaluate the current competencies of your sources of supply and how to extract value from these sources
- Decide what's important for you in your sourcing strategy and how it relates to selecting your technology solution.

17. Dumping Transactions As Soon As Possible.

Nothing bogs down a purchasing department like transactions. It only makes bureaucrats even dumber and more cantankerous. As soon as you can dump transactions and get them out of the purchasing department the better. Use whatever method you can to automate them so that purchasing doesn't even touch them. You don't add any value to them anyway. Key to enabling purchasing to operate at this hyper-pace of relationships is the elimination purchase orders. Here are some good descriptions of the traditional purchasing world realm of purchase orders. Often purchase orders are very laden with steps and totally inefficient. In the traditional bureaucratic purchasing world purchase orders take up over eighty percent of a purchasing professional's time. Often a large percentage of the transactions make up a fraction of the dollars spent. These purchase orders hover around less than two hundred dollars and rarely more than one thousand dollars. Benchmarks of purchase order administrative costs can reach one two hundred and fifty dollars per purchase order. Often payment discounts are missed to suppliers due to the sheer volume of transactions and invoices. Purchase order procedures vary within many companies and there is no rhyme or reason for the rules. Buyers spend over eighty percent of their time being good bureaucrats. There is an accepted norm of perpetual transaction crisis and conflict in the wild paper chase. So called good buyers are often viewed as "super-clerks" who constantly expedite or rush orders. Purchasing is mired in the transaction bayou and basically treading water with alligators perpetually. Alligator wrestling is exhausting and the alligators usually win. Drain the swamp instead.

18. Auctions Are Supplier Hostile Techniques But Appropriate.

Suppliers view auctions as just one time competitive bids. To expect a supplier relationship out of an auction is sheer bonehead folly. Suppliers are just trying to win business at the lowest cost to them. Auctions are at best marginally good for keeping suppliers honest. They work best for mass commodities. Do not expect any long term commitments from suppliers who are successful or any extra added services. If you Wal-Mart your suppliers do not expect any extra added free services.

19. Always Keep the Eye on The Strategy Ball.

Once you deviate from your strategy or principles it is difficult to explain away or rationalize away it to your skeptics. Do not do it. Stick to your guns and your strategy. The need to classify materials and services into particular categories is essential for the success of e-procurement. Each material group may require not only a different procurement strategy but also a different e-procurement or acquisition solution. Companies often try to apply the same vanilla e-procurement strategy across the board to all materials and services. These materials categories demand different strategies, different types of suppliers and different relationships along with the use of multiple tools. Currently e-enabled tools do not exist for certain specific materials needs. They are however rapidly evolving. The placement of a certain materials or services into a particular group may vary by company, industry or a number of factors, depending on the criteria. The key is to have and to articulate a strategy by materials group and to utilise the appropriate tool.

Study the options below. Do not use the dart board approach. Think.

1. Leverage materials strategies include price leverage, the use of competitive bids and long term market agreements. Possible tools include online auctions, E-RFQs, and hedging.

2. Strategic materials strategies include alliances, long term relationships, and alliance contracts. Possible tools include partnering, collaborative design and e-sourcing software.

3. Non-critical materials (MRO) strategies include consolidation, improving logistical costs and

reducing administrative costs. Possible tools include e-procurement software, exchanges, marketplaces and outsourcing storerooms.

4. Bottleneck materials strategies include risk minimization, more inventory, replacement or redesign. Possible tools include value engineering, shared higher inventory, product redesign and collaborative design.

20. Turn Your Strategy into a Dream and Fulfill It.

Get your folks to out dream yourself. Get them to state what the purchasing department of the future will look like and dream and build on that dream. When they out dream you, you know you are on the way to purchasing Shangri-La. Visualize future behaviors and performance. Verbalize them. Verbalize world class behaviors. It helps to ground folks in what you are trying to accomplish. You want them to soar and dream!

21. Picking the Right Metrics. Non-Traditional Ones

Here are my cycle time metrics suggestions. Success in reducing cycle time can be readily measured both quantifiably and qualitatively. As a result, purchasing professionals must ensure that initial cycle-time benchmarking is carefully done before any measurements of success or outcomes are put into place. If you cannot measure it why are you doing it? Here are some of my suggestions for effective cycle-time measurements:

- **On-Time Delivery**

  Enhanced methods to measure on-time delivery include separating components into "A," "B," and "C," categories ("A" being the top priority). Strategic materials must arrive on time. The non strategic material deliveries should be tracked differently. Their purpose is an ancillary supporting role with more delivery leeway being tolerated. To distinguish these categories of delivery, many companies break delivery performance down into these "A," "B," and "C" categories with different percentage goals in each category. One nontraditional measurement is the number of "no-hitch" or perfect deliveries. This means a smooth delivery with zero redundancies and no extra non value-adding work.

- **Inventory Reduction Measurements**

  Measure improved inventory accuracy, labor hours saved taking inventory, elimination of racks, shelves, and materials handling equipment, and reduced maintenance costs. Don't stop here. Many suppliers readily agree to hold materials on a consignment basis. This is a valuable cost-avoidance and cash-flow improvement. Whenever possible, drive to get agreement to pay on consumption. Also, track reductions in supplier inventory. This will help them reduce or hold down their costs to you.

Measure inventory committed to by suppliers and value of materials that are now on consignment or on pay-on-consumption systems. Make note of the various functions or departments that are outsourced. Obtain realistic estimates of the amount of inventory and overhead that would have been required to support these activities if they were not outsourced.

- **Increase in Inventory Turnover**

  Focus your efforts on the "one-touch theory" and the "speed to point of use" for materials or services. Track the number of materials or services touched by only one person in the process right at the point of use or where they are directly needed. Count the total number of transactions processed directly by the end user without any purchasing or middleman interface. A bonus would be that they arrive directly to the end user precisely at the point of use in the manufacturing process. Measure the time it takes for all materials or services to hit your property and get to the point of use.

- **Decrease in Total Cost of Ownership**

  Identify your cost drivers first. These are your significant cost factors that drive the cost of a material or service. Then concentrate on the costs usually reduced or eliminated by faster cycle time but often forgotten in the rush. Measure areas in which processes got simpler and training costs were decreased.

- **Visibility and Appreciation**

  Measure the number of cross-functional teams that purchasing participates in and leads. These can be broken down into three general arenas: design, process, and administrative. Keep records of the number of times other departments come to your department to seek input, advice, and basic participation on strategic planning. Track the number of suppliers that add value to your products at the design stage and the results of their efforts.

- **Increased Integration of Purchasing Strategy into Corporate Strategy**

  Create a five-year strategic plan for purchasing and integrate it into the company's overall strategic plan. Get out into the field with sales and marketing to find out what the final customer really wants in your product, and get the materials and services to meet these needs. Keep track of the number of final customer contacts and the number of changes made because of their input.

- **Increased Cooperation from Suppliers**

  Document all supplier-driven innovations and improvements. Increase and document the number and type of direct links with suppliers, especially direct electronic ties to your production schedule and EDI. Develop in-depth alliance relationships with a few key suppliers at a strategic level to make your quantum leaps in cycle-time reduction. Then measure the success of the alliance by measuring the reduced cycle time. Survey your key suppliers and ask them what they think of the progress of the alliances.

- **Decrease in Manufacturing Cycle Time**

  Keep the tracking of this key parameter simple, to

the point, and at a macro level. Show the number of products or widgets made compared to the cost of goods sold. Thus, if you cut cycle time by 50 percent you should make approximately twice as many widgets with about the same cost of goods sold. Realistically, the cost of goods sold will have to increase, but cycle-time reduction can radically hold down the rate of increase.

- **Purchasing's Internal Customer-Client Satisfaction**

  Start an ongoing internal customer focus team to evaluate the performance and service of purchasing. Periodically use surveys of internal customers, final customers, and suppliers to obtain valuable feedback and direction on how to reduce cycle time. Always include in customer-satisfaction surveys the question, "Has the response time to your request increased, decreased, or stayed the same?" Do not forget face-to-face feedback meetings.

- **Manufacturing Flexibility**

  When measuring flexibility in the manufacturing process, focus on reducing the number of parts. Purchasers can track increases in the number of easily obtainable standardized parts and services with zero lead-time. Suppliers can preassemble and assist in these types of efforts.

  Do not neglect the administrative cycle time in a purchasing department -- whether you work for a manufacturing company or a service organization. Purchasers can set cycle-time standards in their departments and streamline all procedures to speed things up. For example, procurement cards and system-purchasing systems can help reduce cycle time. With these 10 measurements, your efforts to reduce cycle time will become focused and can be easily understood by your customers and suppliers. Use them as much as feasible.

Some more measurements you should consider. If you can't measure it why do it?

Some of my Additional Possible Non-Traditional Measures for Procurement to Be Noted:

- The number of preferred suppliers under long term contract
- The number of supplier alliance relationships
- The number of single source parts, commodities, services
- The number of suppliers providing on site service
- The number of new products or design reviews that suppliers participated in on a team
- The number of transaction's processed direct by the end-user
- The number and dollar value of mutual cost reductions with suppliers
- The number and dollar volume of purchase card purchases
- The number of cross functional teams that purchasing professionals are contributing members
- The dollar value on continuous replenishment stocking plans
- The percent of purchasing personnel pursuing an advanced degree
- The number of continuing education hours or seminar hours by purchasing personnel
- The percentage of purchasing professionals certified
- The number of suppliers registered to ISO-9000

- The number of suppliers with direct links to us
- The number of active suppliers
- The average lead-time of purchased components and parts
- The cycle time or velocity of delivery of our equipment to the customer
- Cycle time from sales order placement to purchased part acquisition
- Creation and updating of a 5 year strategic purchasing plan

There is more than enough significant metrics and justification available for non traditional procurement. The challenge is selling the concept to top management. Usually and unfortunately they are more interested in bottom line impacts for the next quarterly report.

22. How to Avoid Dragging Out the RFP Process.

Always set a final deadline for returning an RFI or RFP. If a supplier does not meet the deadline don't consider them. Don't ever compromise a bid or the bid process by favoring certain suppliers. Many folks want to procrastinate bids. The real reason is their stake in a relationship with their homey supplier is threatened. They feel that they may be proven dead wrong especially if their favorite son supplier falters. If suppliers can't follow basic instructions on RFPs do you really want them in a relationship? I think not.

23. Just Go With Your Gut On Some Suppliers.

Cultural fit and chemistry is important. If the relationship is strictly going to be commercial and not a true partnership it is fine to go with you gut on some supplier selections. Make sure they have the capabilities to grow with you. Gut check time is scary for some folks but it is okay to go with your gut on some suppliers.

24. Supplier Site Visits Are a Must.

You can tell a great deal about a person by visiting their home and surroundings. This also holds true for suppliers. Check out the attitude of employees, housekeeping, professionalism and facilities. Never ever enter a serious partnership with a supplier without visiting their main plants or facilities. Do not be afraid to go off tour and talk to other employees. You will learn a great deal about their culture and their capabilities. Most folks are honest about who they work for when asked in a non-threatening manner. You will be surprised at what you learn from such conversations.

25. Make Transaction Experiences Super User Friendly Or Else It Will Fail.

Face it, internal folks view doing their own procurement transactions as an outright pain. Every effort must be made to make them simple, intuitive and painless. Catalogues must be super-simple. Catalogue content is a key. Time is of the essence to anyone buying. One of the reasons the Russian empire fell was not Star Wars but because so many people had to wait so long in so many lines in order to buy so few basically worthless goods. Waiting riles people up. Target a transaction completion for 30 seconds or less. If you can archive previous requisitions that folks can copy, cut and paste quickly into new ones by all means employ this tactic. Do not waste their time on busy work. Their time is valuable.

26. Keep Routine Buys Simple. Do Not Bureaucracy.

Don't add layers of audits, logs, paperwork and other drivel to simple routine buys for Pete's sake. Most of this stuff is not necessary for folks to do their jobs. Don't add layers of bureaucracy to "protect" the company. Small purchase orders are small chump change stuff. Concentrate on the strategic stuff. This is where the folding money is. Many companies have so many restrictions on small dollar value transactions that don't make sense. They bend over to pick up the pennies while the paper bills or folding money flies right away. Let it go. Trust your employees to do small purchase orders.

27. Just How Many Strategic Suppliers and How to Select Them.

Strategic sourcing is a disciplined process organizations implement in order to more efficiently purchase goods and services from suppliers. The goal is to reduce total acquisition cost while improving value. A Strategic sourcing strategy should be initiated immediately. A comprehensive sourcing methodology should be followed religiously to include strategic alliance and strategic relationship building with key suppliers. Key supplier alliances must be established. Supplier rationalization (reduction) must be accomplished first and dramatically. Many consulting firms offer a Strategic Sourcing Management solution that walks online users through each step of a consulting-type procurement methodology, including gathering data, analyzing requirements, and setting strategy, as well as executing e-procurement through shopping e-marketplaces, conducting reverse auctions, and using other methods built into the application.

Here is a Strategic Sourcing Step Process that outlines an iterative six-step process:

- Assess Opportunity
- Assess Internal Supply Chain
- Assess Supply Markets
- Develop Sourcing Strategy
- Implement Strategy
- Institutionalize Strategy

The activities within each step may appear to be performed in sequence, but in fact *this is not reality*. Over the course of the process, the sourcing teams may often revisit the steps and revise their approach.

Here are just some of the key benefits to addressing strategic sourcing and procurement.

- Reduction of overall costs equals centralized, negotiated contracts and streamlined procurement process, take advantage of all available discounts.
- Increased communications about products equals improved use of technology.
- Reduced number of suppliers equals stronger

relationships/partnerships with suppliers resulting in a more flexible and responsive supply pipeline that is managed proactively instead of reactively.

- Increased purchasing efficiency equals use of e-commerce applications and procurement cards.
- Reduced purchased unit costs
- Reduced acquisition costs
- Increased inventory turnover
- Improved downstream operations equals higher quality shipments, on time, the right components in the right quantities

Supplier alliances or partnerships are critical for any e-procurement success. In addition the e-procurement readiness for these suppliers must be assessed rigorously and tested. All too often suppliers give only lip service to e-procurement capabilities. Their customers must insist on the testing of supplier e-procurement and catalogue capabilities. Suppliers must be assessed to see if they are ready for e-procurement. Capabilities must be measured and references from other companies sought out to ensure that the chosen suppliers could deal with e-procurement. Strong consideration should be given to dividing or segmenting suppliers into tiers of capability such as Tiers 1-2-3. Supplier integration with back office systems is also a strong criterion. Alliances should only be formed with suppliers who can offer some sort of a significant competitive edge or who cover and reduce major purchasing dollars.

The supplier relationship is where the traditional and the progressive purchasing differ the most. The traditional is a short term approach, adversary based and mostly hands off commercial. Serious cost cutting is rare. Communication is usually at arms length. Shopping is continuous charade and purchasing is perpetually hunting for a better "deal". The world is one big strip mall of suppliers. The low bidder often wins the bid. The norm is three quotes and the required blizzard of paperwork for a cheap supplier. The atmosphere is one of low trust, weak commitment and supplier long term performance is often not monitored well or at all. Expediting of parts is a continuous three ring circus. More modern supplier relationships are geared towards the long term at least three to five years. Close collaboration is open with the mutual sharing of plans, design, goals and rewards. The lowest total cost of ownership is valued and value-adding services are the norm. Suppliers are empowered to just get it done. The so-called iceberg of supplier opportunity clearly explains that only five to ten percent of efficiency is gained via price, and it is the area of least resistance and work. The ninety to ninety-five percent of the so-called new frontier of supplier exploration is actual bottom line total cost of ownership savings of utilizing a preferred supplier. This is the one area of the greatest resistance and opportunity. This is the realm of relationship building that requires increasing communication and the building of trust.

Flexibility in supplier relationship building is a must. Use the 80-20 rule. Concentrate on building relationships with suppliers that you spend the most dollars on. Develop strategic relationships with suppliers only who will give you a distinct competitive advantage to your paying or end-user customers. Most corporations can only manage a few of these critical relationships. They must be at the highest level with executive and other personnel exchanges. The other low value or miscellaneous materials do not need strong relationship efforts. These relationships can remain strictly commercial. There is no need to waste precious resources on developing relationships with these suppliers. Steer clear of the emotional materials at first. Many people in companies develop personal relationships with suppliers. People love trinkets, dinners, golf, and personal attention, etc. from suppliers. Unfortunately this doesn't drive money to the company's bottom line. Do not underestimate this personal factor. Identify your key suppliers early. If anyone in your organization has had prior reengineering experience use him or her as much as possible. Reengineering is often an endurance contest where the last man or woman (gladiator) left standing wins. The problem is many individuals dig in and hope to wear the reengineering team out. Reengineering is a marathon not a sprint. Do not be afraid to lose some minor battles initially in order to win the war. The long haul is a long haul.

Understanding paying customer needs drives the process. Note or list internal customer needs only. Concentrate on what counts to the ultimate paying customers. How do we find this out? Ask them! Supplier receptiveness to the relationships and the change process needs to be carefully and slowly pursued. Top management needs to understand that resistance will be fierce and some individuals will not change and must be dealt with appropriately. Accounting needs to re-think the way it keeps score. Standard cost based systems are too antiquated to adequately report on progress for this process. Activity based accounting is much more suited to the reengineering process and the correct assessment of progress. Always strive for the highest performance with clear vision and clear objectives. Internal customers or end-users that previously were not permitted to perform transactions or even dialogue with suppliers now must be seamlessly connected. Purchasing must get out of the worthless middle-person syndrome. Purchasing needs to forego its role as a rule throwing contract imbedding obstructionist. The organization must constantly be flexible and look forward to upgrades. Markets change so must procurement. Get on your track shoes and keep ahead of the market.

28. Trial Periods for Suppliers Some Advice.

During trial periods new suppliers are most vulnerable to naysayers and attackers. Make sure you meet frequently with them. You need to act almost with SWAT team efficiency when a problem occurs and solve it immediately. Agree to problem solving procedures in advance and deadlines. Solve glitches and explain what happened openly. This is not the time for shoving things under the rug or stonewalling problems. Fix them on the spot whenever possible.

29. Why Procurement Folks Do Not Want To Give Up "Their" Relationships.

Many end-users have personal stakeholder relationships in certain suppliers and the relationships developed over the years with these suppliers. A change transformation plan must be established to deal with the evolution to new relationships with new suppliers. Use a change management model to address these issues and ensure the acceptance of any e-procurement initiative. Breaking up is hard to do as the song says but it must be done and done quickly.

30. Know Best Practices but Use Common Sense

Know and be an apostle of best practices. Make sure they are sound and have been tested. Focus on your own industries procurement best practices. Always use your gut and experience to sanity check best practices and their applicability to your company. This cannot be taught, but it is very necessary. Keep researching best practices and keep them current.

Herb using his "gut" to check best practices

31. Expect Murphy To Strike. Be Ready.

New systems and new suppliers are certain to *not* be perfect. Make sure you rehearse as much as possible any new systems or procedures. Test and test again. Communicate and make sure feedback sessions are scheduled. Fix it with a sense of urgency. Murphy and his law can be overcome. Be ready to deal with it. Have a problem solving procedure mapped in advance. Follow it.

32. Get Quick Wins.

People and teams need reinforcement. Always go for the simple quick little wins and make sure to publicize the little wins quickly. You will be surprised how little wins can snowball into big wins. Celebrate them. Build that momentum.

33. Run a Marketing Campaign That Would Make Madison Avenue Jealous.

Establishing a strong communication plan for your e-procurement or procurement transformation project is critical for its success. Seeking help from trained marketing professionals and communication experts is essential. A continuous communication plan utilizing various media will help overcome the resistance to change. You cannot over communicate. An example of a communications plan I used is listed below:

Example Communications Plan:

- Continue to educate top management on the strategic importance of supply management and e-procurement
- Conduct a surveys of suppliers and publish the results to end-users
- Conduct an internal customer surveys and act on the concerns
- Provide continuing advanced purchasing education for selected key end-users
- Conduct quarterly reviews with key suppliers and publish the results
- Conduct quarterly open purchasing forums with a town hall format
- Publish a purchasing newsletters
- Conduct joint supplier roundtable discussions as required and open to end-users
- Bring in suppliers to solve design, standardization, and administration problems
- Update the Purchasing Information Manual as required

- Publish monthly letters from purchasing department
- Start visible tracking of purchasing goals
- Target selected e-mail news to end-users
- Create a e-procurement news web site
- Encourage the formation of a e-procurement power user news group

34. Admit Supplier Selection Mistakes Quickly and Deselect.

It's painful and expensive, but you must shoot that bad supplier racehorse immediately if the fit is not there. Usually when the strategic selection process is short circuited or not fully employed a supplier mistake is made. It is more the fault of not doing the homework or following the process. Other failure causes are inability to establish a true relationship. Again this is a hard process to predict or quantify. Admit the mistake, finalize the divorce and then reexamine the process of selection. Deselect then reselect.

35. Bureaucracy Dies Hard. Put a Stake In Its Heart.

Bureaucracy can never be successfully downsized or reduced. It must be obliterated with a passion or it will come back with a vengeance and retrench itself. Always go for elimination of bureaucracy. Take no prisoners. Salt the bureaucracy earth. Don't modify or adjust. Destroy.

36. Standardize Equipment and Services.

Engineers always have their pets and biases. We all do. It is critical to get them on cross functional teams to standardize parts and equipment. A goal of 80% standardized parts is realistic in many industries. Difference in brands (suppliers), OEMs, and parts must have significant added value to be justified. Try to measure quality with an obscure balkanization of OEMs and different parts (ha). Good luck. The same holds for services. Standardize them. One of the guiding principles of industrialization is standardization. Do not lose sight of it! Pursue it. Standardize whenever possible.

37. Slay The Sacred Cows Quickly. Convert Them Into Sacred Steaks.

I once worked for a company with a seven part purchase order form and every purchase order had to be approved by the Vice President of Finance. People were so disheartened by the abysmal speed of the system that maverick ways of purchasing were rampart. We went to a two part short order form for everything under $500 and eventually to purchase cards. We eliminated seven file cabinets of forms. People had confidence in the systems and were much more truthful in expressing their needs. The Vice President of Finance had more time to get IPO funding and ensure our financial viability not deciding who should be purchasing pens and pencils. Be super aggressive with transaction reduction. No one will mourn for them when they are gone.

38. If You Don't Ask You Don't Get. So Ask.

My key rule of negotiations is to ask, ask and ask. Do not be afraid to ask for anything from a supplier or fellow departments. They cannot meet your needs is they do not realize what they are. Asking also flatters them. You will be pleasantly surprised at what you get. Ask.

39. Total Cost of Ownership. Good Luck Getting Buy In.

Most folks don't understand total cost of ownership or concepts like activity based costing. They are still mired in the "Price is King" world. They can not get past price. Always map out the total cost of a supply chain especially if resistance to change is strong. Try to calculate the costs of various steps, transformations and non value add stuff. Do your research. Explain total costs.

40. Visibility Is Key To Tracking Progress. Keep It Clear and Simple.

Show folks how you are doing versus you metrics. Use

pictures and graphics. People can relate to them much better. Spreadsheets are not very publicity friendly. Do not be shy with graphs and always display them professionally. Keep the radar gun on the process and suppliers. Let other folks see the results good and bad.

41. How to Retrain Remove or Fire Uncooperative Purchasing Folks

Many purchasing folks can't adapt and they die hard or resist with a vengeance. Some are recalcitrant kamikazes bent on destroying the new procurement process. There is no easy way to convert them. Start the process to put them on an improvement plan no matter how painful and time consuming it is. The rest of the folks need to know that you are serious about behavior changes. Stick to your guns. Get human resources help. It is an endurance contest so don't falter or flinch. They will kick and scream. Like a good parent you can outlast any tantrum.

42. It's About Leverage and Being Consistent. Keep the Stories Straight.

Leverage anything you can with a supplier. It just isn't about price but also about services that they can provide you. Whatever you leverage from a supplier make sure all your folks understand what you have leveraged and consistently tell the success story across the enterprise. Keep the stories straight and consistent. Do not exaggerate leverage savings. Keep them simple and understandable.

43. Rope In Maverick Buyers. How to Knock 'Um Dead.

Shoot a few maverick crows first. When a maverick buy occurs it can not be ignored. Punishment must be swift and unfortunately brutal. Examples are necessary. Don't be shy about being Attila the Hun with maverick buyers. It pays off. The rest of the crows fall in line very quickly.

44. Why Everyone Thinks They Are A Better Negotiator Than You. They Could Have Got A Better Deal Mania.

For some reason just about everyone not in purchasing thinks they are better shoppers or buyers than purchasing. They feel that they can always get a better deal. Often in traditional purchasing they could, but the additional transaction costs of their so called maverick deals were killers. Rather than fight them educate them and even put the most vocal so called better deal makers or shoppers on cross functional teams that source suppliers. Use that energy and redirect it.

45. Standardize Terms, Conditions, and Contracts, Hew the Boilerplate.

Why have hundreds of different terms with suppliers, contracts, agreements, etc. Suppliers love confusion and non standard approaches. Boilerplate what ever you can. Any contract that takes more than 30 days to put in place is not worth doing. Lawyers, bureaucrats and fools always think that somehow a contract will "protect" them or the company. Relationships are not built on the thickness of the pages of a massive contract. Trust must come first, not legal "I dotting". He you hides behind a contract needs high life insurance. Contracts will not save you from adversarial relationships. Contracts encourage adversary.

46. Establishing Beachheads and How to Take the Beach.

Pilots are good for certain purchasing ventures but don't procrastinate or extend them out ad infinitum. It is a good way for the resistance to kill you off. The burden of proof is 51% or reasonable. It is not beyond a reasonable doubt or a 12-0 unanimous jury vote. If you use the later criteria you will never have a successful pilot. Make sure one person is accountable for the beachhead and can understand the total picture. Folks love experiments but remember the first rule of experiments is to have controls!

47. How to Dethrone Price as King.

Any supplier can low ball on the price of any item. Retail stores are great at having lead in low price items in one aisle with the marked up high margin items very near. Always benchmark prices whenever possible with other companies. Keep a handle on the price pulse. When a supplier offers a low ball price see if they can extend the percent price decrease to all your other items from them. Usually dead silence results or the quick back peddling begins.

48. Pick the Best Suppliers or You Will Not Be the Best Company.

The Porter model is a powerful tool that can be used in the supplier selection and understanding the process. It is a systematic approach to market analysis which is often-used by marketing. The goal here is industry analysis and to enable purchasing to know as much or more about an industry than a supplier who is participating in that industry. This tool reinforces the maxim that he or she who has the most information in negotiations has the advantage. Believe it. Knowledge is power. Shoe pounding and other adversarial tactics are typical for theatre and opera but not purchasing.

49. Get That Cycle Time for Big Gains

You will be amazed about how much of cycle time is fluff or queues. Often reducing cycle time is just getting rid of the padding or conservative Cover Your Butt stuff folks build into it. Significant gains can be made without spending a dime. Procedure elimination or cutting out the non value stuff can yield big gains. When people don't have accurate or timely information they pad cycle time to reduce their personal risk.

50. Change Everyone's Role and Insist That They Play a New Role.

The third "R" in the reengineering process is the realignment of roles. Cross-function teams need to be the norm. Purchasing personnel will spend more and more time outside of their department or area which is precisely where they belong. Unless the purchasing leader is comfortable with this new arrangement the new way of doing business with be severely hampered. Intensive coaching of many simultaneously running teams and tracking their progress will be necessary. Suppliers can also assume some of the role of R&D and not think in a vacuum when proposing improvement to materials, parts or services.

51. How to Fight Kicking and Screaming Tactics.

Like kids use time outs for the screamers. Make sure you explain that you will not tolerate such tactics. Don't be afraid to walk out of a meeting when they are used. Confront the behavior first and do not tolerate it. If it persists pull the trigger.

52. Use A Roadmap. Stick To It. Use A Compass.

Here is a good roadmap shortlist I have used for E-procurement
- BPR-Reengineering-"As is" assessment
- Strategic Sourcing
- Supplier Rationalization
- Supplier Alliances and the selection of the best of the best
- Metrics and justification
- Data Catalogue normalization
- E-procurement tools selection
- Marketing-Communication Plan
- Change Transformation

53. Beware Of Bean Counter Logic. It Will Derail the Process.

Many accountants can't get beyond price. Their accounting systems can't measure soft or activity-based costs. They always want to see so called hard results. They like to audit incessantly. Don't let them rule. Keep pushing back on their logic and justification. No one ever brought a share of stock because of so called world class accounting systems.

54. Enforce Rules. Again Bushwhack The First Crows That Fly Off The Fence. Kapow!

Governance, rules and discipline in buying is essential. Folks that violate the rules must be dealt with quickly and the workforce needs to realize the consequences. Again the first crows that jump off the fence need to be taken care of quickly. Put the weapon on auto fire. Kapow! Maverick buying will soon dry up.

55. Introduce Discipline.

Purchasing and transaction discipline are critical. Most folks do not like it but much of the routine purchases and process must be disciplined. Discipline especially around using preferred suppliers must be strictly enforced. Make folks e-savvy and using catalogues. Teach them how to search catalogues or they will soon quit searching.

56. Reject All Non-Value Adding Work. Be a Non-Value Refusenik.

Shed all non value work quickly. Get rid of it. Don't add any and don't encourage purchasing folks to reinvent any. Do not do any additional work unless it is justified by savings. Do not document for the sake of documentation. Nobody reads it anyway.

57. Trust Everyone But Cut The Cards. Be Prudent.

Trust everyone until they give you reason not to trust them. Cut the cards however. Be prudent but not overly concerned with tracking every transaction. Suppliers need to know that you are tracking their performance, and you will take action if they falter.

58. Overcoming the Auditing To Ad Finitum Logic

Don't agree to any additional audits or audit tactics. Make auditors justify their additional audit requirements by proving how much money it will save or value it will add. No justification no audit. Does it save anything? Prove it.

59. Defusing the Sour Grapes of Deselected Suppliers. Hell Hath No Fury Like A Supplier Scorned.

Often disgruntled suppliers will sow seeds of doubt especially when a new supplier is selected. Best advice is to totally ban them from your property and all further contact with the company. Purchasing should have the first and last say on which suppliers are even allowed on company property. Don't back down on this issue. Backdoor purchasing by other departments especially engineering is rampant in many companies. Nip it in the bud. Punish the "back door bugga Lou" dancers.

60. Procurement Résistance Is Fierce Do Not Underestimate It. The Fifth Column Effect

By far the biggest barrier to reengineering purchasing is the enormous and overwhelming fear of change. Dr. Demming was right when he cited the need to drive out fear. A severe job security issue among purchasing professionals often helps create an atmosphere of fear that is nearly impossible to overcome. Before the undertaking of the journey of reengineering of purchasing an assessment of where purchasing professionals are on their career path-cycle and in their approach is essential. The four milestones along the path are beginners or start-up, adapters or maintenance, risk takers or innovators and visionary or leading edge. Purchasing professionals can be classified as reactive, mechanical, proactive and American Keirestsu. The reactive state is the typical fire fighting jumping to operating crisis mode of many departments. The mechanical mode is the super-bureaucrat that has mastered the inefficient system. The proactive state shows spurts of planning and some significant progress. Often it is haphazard. The American Keirestu is the end state of supply management prowess. The key here is to re-skill people and provide the training to lead the reengineering process.

End-users (internal buyers) demand ease of use and they want to quickly find the items that they need. Companies need to realize that e-procurement is competing with the easiest method to buy in the minds of their end-users. Many end-users would rather pick up a phone, tell their supplier what items they want, charge it to a corporate purchase card and hang up. Unfortunately in many companies this method is still faster then using the current e-procurement software. Any impediments to the fast purchase of materials will quickly turn off end-users and kill transaction volumes. Speed is king in the world of e-procurement. End-users also want powerful search engines to quickly find their items. If the content supplier catalogue is poorly organised and the quality poor, end-users will quickly be frustrated by unfruitful searches and become non-users of the e-procurement system. In addition special instructions that need to be given to suppliers about delivery or other issues can't easily be given with some e-procurement tools or require additional end-user training which raises the frustration levels.

Finally there is the relationship factor with new suppliers. Often new suppliers are installed for indirect materials solely because they seem to have more e-procurement capabilities. End-users value relationships with suppliers that they have trusted over the years. E-procurement is highly impersonal and web based. Resistance to change for an e-procurement system is fierce but can be readily overcomes with strong commitment to change management. This change management process must be an integral part of any e-procurement installation. Never underestimate the role resistance to change plays in this transformation. There are three sayings to be aware of when e-procurement is implemented:

Shift happens. Change is constant. Emotion rules logic.

61. Know the Politics of Some Supplier Selections and Adjust To It.

If the CEO is a golf buddy with one of your current suppliers; face reality, you are probably not going to dislodge them. Make sure they are not strategic. Do not lose the war just because of an unimportant battle.

62. Cross Functional Teams. Do Not Get Teamed To Death.

Cross functional teams work but make sure teams are doing meaningful work. If your purchasing professionals are not on cross functional teams they are not in the program. Make sure teams have deadlines for results.

63. Understand BPR Reengineering and it's Limitations.

Do not put a lot of faith in the "as is" of business process engineering. You usually will not learn much from your antiquated existing practices. Find out the best practices and strive for them. Dream do not reminiscence.

64. Pick Your Alliances Wisely but Go At Them with a Passion.

Focus on just a few alliances. You can only have deep alliance relationships with a few suppliers. Make sure you can get a competitive advantage from the alliance. Alliances take a lot of effort and time. Make sure they have the potential to pay off.

65. Select the Right E-Tools for the Right Situations

Here are some pertinent tips on selecting e-tools:

- Research all the alternatives: Potential solutions include a variety of alternatives: Internet, intranet, extranet, application service provider (ASP), server-based, ERP, stand-alone, exchanges, and B2B hubs. Find an industry source that is not vested in the ultimate decision choice and use its knowledge to develop the list of viable alternatives.

- Define points of integration: Working with IT and relevant support units defines those potential points of integration necessary to capitalize on information and systems investments already made. Some examples include human resources, general ledger, accounts payable, fixed assets, inventory, asset management, and help desk applications.

- Document business needs: The ideal solution for each organization may differ based upon the activities planned to flow through the system, commodities and services to be acquired, business practices, industry and legacy system requirements, and department or initiative budgets.

- Issue a request for information (RFI): Use the submissions to gain a much greater understanding of the offerings available in the marketplace, and to refine the system requirements.
- Eliminate unacceptable options: Drop from consideration any option that does not fall within acceptable IT parameters. If the proposed solution is incompatible with the organization infrastructure or business objectives, eliminate it. Focus on solutions that require minimal effort to integrate effectively within the planned environment.

66. Integrate Procurement with Other Departments.

Break down your stovepipe and put procurement folks in other departments. Force them to understand other department needs. Let them go to production meetings and participate. Encourage them to explain to folks what they are doing. Get them on the front lines not the rear bureaucracy. Let them wander about and learn the business. There is not much real business knowledge learned in a cubicle.

67. Materials Experts or Product Experts?

The final customer wants the total product to satisfy them. Material experts are valuable but the customer expects the total product to perform. Purchasing folks need both the commodity and material expertise and a firm understanding of what the final customer really values in the product. They must become customer centric first.

68. Where Should Procurement Be In The Organization? Get In the Right Sandbox.

Procurement or supply chain folks need their own organization or vice president. They represent more that 50% of the cost of goods sold. They are too critical to the success of a company to report to another function. They need to be in their own sandbox and invite others into the sandbox.

69. Head Off The Lawyers. Get Them To Standardize Contracts With You. Set Page Limits.

Lawyers are good delayers of contracts. They love to play tit for tat with suppliers. Get them involved in boiler plating contracts for various goods and services. Hold them to page and word limits for contracts. Make sure common sense language prevails not legalese.

70. Ask Your Suppliers For Advice. What a Novel Concept.

Many suppliers have years of experience with many customers and have seen best practices utilized. Ask them frequently for advice and act upon it. Suppliers are one of the best sources of innovation. They don't have your corporate politics to stifle them. Many know what has worked for other companies.

71. Pay Procurement Folks For Performance Not Paper Shuffling.

Pay purchase folks on how well they do with their commodities, materials or services. They must beat the market they are dealing with. If the market prices went down 5% during the year they need to do better than a 5 % price reduction. Make them market focused first. Don't make them focus on bureaucratic stuff.

72. Eliminate Fire Fighting. Do Not Glamorize It.

Crises victims love good fire fighters. If purchasing folks are involved in too many tactical firefights they are not doing their jobs especially strategically or they have chosen the wrong suppliers. Do not reward good fire fighters it just encourages short term fire fighting behavior. Prevention of fires must be valued. Ask Smokey the Bear. He will concur.

73. How to Sell Procurement Cards (My article).

Procurement cards are a proven best practice. Card providers are constantly upgrading their systems, reports, and software, and continuously improving the functionality of the cards. So why are so many purchasing departments unable to implement a procurement- card program? There are many reasons; including that implementing procurement cards can demand an outstanding internal sales program and intense persuasion of your internal customers. If this is the case in your organization, brush up on your sales skills. One of the biggest barriers to implementing a procurement-card program is selling the concept internally. Such a crucial sell requires excellent sales and marketing skills. The good news is that these skills can be learned. Here are some guidelines to help you sell the procurement-card program.

74. Some of my Procurement Card Pre-Work Tips

The following is some pre-work to complete before your presentation to sell the concept:
- Target your savings. Get a good projection on the number of transactions that will be eliminated and exactly what items can be purchased with the cards. Get the hard savings calculated right first including reductions in mailing, checks, time, and forms.
- Establish in advance which suppliers will accept the procurement card. This will help eliminate initial teething pains with inexperienced suppliers.
- Establish a transaction cost and include it in your savings. Many accounting and consulting firms can calculate this cost for you and boost the credibility of your savings.

- Involve as many parties as possible in the pre-work stage, especially accounting and receiving. If possible, conduct site visits to firms that have successfully implemented procurement-card programs and arrange face-to-face meetings with the accounting and receiving departments to help your internal people understand the concept, learn from their experiences, and alleviate their fears.

75. Purchase Cards Two Biggest Fears.

The two biggest fears that you need to deal with are control and security fraud. During your "sales" presentation, make sure you present all the safeguards against fraud. Control is one of the strongest selling points of procurement cards. Contrast the elaborate controls available with procurement cards as compared with your current small-purchase control system. If you don't address and eliminate these two fears from every angle possible, you will not sell the procurement-card program. Enlist a champion, preferably at the vice president or director level, to understand the procurement-card program and assist you in the implementation.

76. Target Key Groups for Purchase Cards.

Target your controller and key accountants for even more persuasion. Listen carefully to their concerns and address them. Constant reassurance of the "best practice nature" concept of the procurement card can be accomplished via some pre-sell methods such as meetings with key requisitioners, alliances with maintenance personnel who usually become the procurement card's strongest proponents, and finding out if your competitors are using procurement cards. Ask your suppliers if they are willing to give personal testimonials about procurement cards and how the transaction data is gathered at their site.

77. Fine-Tune the Purchase Card Presentation.

Limit your presentation to no more than 30 minutes. Be specific about your rollout plan, objectives, goals, savings, and impact on other departments. Be prepared to answer the tough questions about control and security fraud. The procurement-card concept is a strategic tool that can help purchasing professionals escape the paperwork swamp. Preparation and marketing are essential for procurement card acceptance in your organization. Concentrate your resources in these two areas and your sales presentation should be well- received.

78. Some More Tips for Procurement Cards.

Credit-card purchases by end-users (your internal customers) can be one of the win-win results of reengineering purchasing. With these direct purchases, end-users are empowered to purchase routine or necessary items. Many purchasing departments clearly see these tremendous transaction cost savings but aren't sure how to train end-users to purchase directly with procurement cards or via other methods. The simplest and most effective way to implement this empowerment is to publish a purchasing information manual designed just for them.

79. Develop a Purchase Card Purchasing Manual? What is the purpose?

The manual's primary purpose should be to give down-to-earth "nuts and bolts" instructions. Give clear pointers with concrete examples. Make sure card users receive some basic ethical ground rules and a written company policy on gifts and gratuities, and help them get familiar with rudimentary contract law. Make sure you have the entire purchasing department contribute to the manual. Other key internal departments such as accounting, accounts payable, and receiving can also provide valuable input to further streamline the transaction cycle.

80. What should be the contents of the Purchase card manual?

Try to keep the manual brief and to the point. Limit the number of pages. Three-ring binders provide the option of quickly adding and removing information in the future. Open the manual with a table of contents and divide it into sections via labeled tabs or dividers. The manual should include a purchasing organizational chart and the specific responsibilities of purchasers. Provide a glossary of typical purchasing terms and some basic purchasing policies and goals, along with emergency contacts. Have a section where purchasing newsletters or flyers can be accumulated, and insert a feedback form in each manual that can be sent to purchasing with end-user suggestions.

81. How to give the details on corporate purchasing cards.

Encourage end-users to use procurement cards first whenever possible. Draw analogies to using a personal credit card. List the names and telephone numbers of in-house administrators, along with the 1-800 telephone help numbers of your purchase-card provider. Provide examples of internal control forms and suppliers a list of preferred who accept the cards. Give specific examples of what to do when items are to be returned or a charge is disputed. Pre qualify suppliers by having purchasing actually perform at least one purchase via the corporate purchasing card and reviewing all the subsequent reports.

82. How to Organize the Purchase card roll-out.

If possible; publicize the manual's roll-out in your purchasing or company newsletter. Have a formal kick-off meeting with the entire purchasing team present. Give out the manual at training sessions. Provide smaller training classes for the key end-users so questions can be answered before the manual is used. Inform your key preferred suppliers about the manual, and give them copies if they desire. Prepare suppliers for the end-user procurement card purchases, alerting them that questions may arise from the end-users. All the manuals should be numbered and an issue log kept so that you know who has been issued a copy. A master copy should be kept in a safe place with pending updates and revisions nearby.

83. How to Follow-up to the Purchase card manual.

Every member of the purchasing department should have a copy of the manual. When internal customers arrive in the department with questions, purchasing department members should sit down with them and guide them to the answers in the manual. A purchasing information manual is one aspect of training employees' companywide for procurement-card use.

84. Some Pitfalls for Procurement Cards.

Just about any supplier or business will accept them. Some employees will abuse them. Be prepared to deal with them immediately. Purchase card transaction information is often vague or incomplete. My best advice is to limit or only use them with a group of preferred trusted suppliers.

85. Can Change Of This Magnitude Be Controlled or Just Wave Ridden?

Go with the flow. You cannot completely control a major change process. There will be setbacks and things will have to be revisited. We do not always catch the perfect wave when surfing. When you fall off the board get back on. Control freaks will not be able to deal with major change.

86. Treat Your Time like a Precious Rare Earth Element

Do not get sucked into endless meetings. Put suppliers first. They will make or break you. Market your plans with a passion and never compromise your integrity. Do not give up your time unless the benefits are measurable and big. Avoid time sinks. Prioritize relationships not paperwork.

87. Why Try E-Procurement?

A Company must focus on its current business or procurement practices first before trying e-procurement. For many companies these still remain very archaic and transaction intensive. The process of the reengineering of purchasing is an excellent first step in achieving the full benefits of e-procurement. This is where a comprehensive procurement assessment is mandatory. (The "as is" state). Companies can do a gap analysis and offers a spend assessment to help in this area. Standardized purchasing processes and rules are essential preceding steps. Procurement procedures should be clearly defined along with current supplier relationship depth. E-procurement is a powerful tool but a disciplined procurement approach should be in place before e-procurement solutions are implemented. The procurement must come before the e. unfortunately many companies do not have good information on procurement spend, transactions, commodities and suppliers, which makes an assessment extremely difficult.

Before establishing metrics and justification for e-procurement a familiarity with supply chain best practices must be established. Some Supply Chain Best Practices include the measurements from the following bullets:

- Form strategic alliances with suppliers, service vendors and shippers
- Facilitate information sharing by giving them input in strategies, plans and product development
- Facilitate greater information sharing of demand, product design and development data at multiple levels of the organization
- Reduce the number of regular suppliers by shifting to single sourcing, to shorten cycle times for development and to cut costs
- Review suppliers' performance on multiple criteria, such as ISO9000 and Malcolm Baldrige, as well as process criteria
- Implement VMI (Vendor Managed Inventory): the automatic or continuous replenishment of a customer's inventory by the supplier, based on product stocking model parameters and POS data

- Change working attitude from an adversarial relationship to a partnership relationship
- Process is completely electronic - many companies have links with customers and suppliers and within company between systems
- Tools to allow understanding of tradeoffs for investment buying (carrying costs, algorithms, etc.)
- Provide demand information to suppliers (such as consumer demand as well as customer demand)
- Strong relationship with few suppliers
- Consolidation
- Leveraged buying
- Intranet-based catalogs
- Internet-based purchasing
- Procurement cards

88. Specific E-procurement Justification Metrics.

Consider these metrics
- *Reducing* the time employees spend purchasing, whether it's leafing through catalogues or surfing the Web.
- *Leveraging* their volume with preferred suppliers in order to get better pricing, service, and access to new technology.
- *Limiting* choices to only those suppliers, materials, and services that they are confident can meet pre-approved levels of price and quality.

An additional benefit of these approaches is reducing cycle times for responding to ongoing or unanticipated business needs. In many companies, the total elapsed time required to requisition even standard items is often weeks — resulting in manufacturing downtime or inefficiency while waiting for materials, or carrying higher buffer stocks of "just in case" inventories. Using e-procurement tools to streamline and speed up the process, these cycle times can typically be reduced to a matter of days or even hours. For efficiency-related changes, the direct impact on the bottom line is often hard to measure. For example, purchasing and administrative overhead costs really only decrease if total staff levels are reduced. If all you do is cut the number of purchase orders in half and leave your staffing at the same level, then the cost to process one simply goes up from $200 to $400. More frequently, staffs are reassigned to projects and activities that have higher potential value to the company but were previously not addressed. Determining the real business value of these efficiency-related e-procurement solutions requires asking the question "What new things are we doing now that we are freed from this administrative burden, and what the measurable value to the organization is?" Frankly, the answer is often not well known or not really planned out.

89. Additional Benefits List for E-Procurement:

Examine these additional possible benefits.

- Improve productivity organization wide through streamlining the purchasing process and reducing cycle times. Reported results include 50 to 70 percent improvement in cycle times from an average of 7.3 days for fulfillment to two days.
- Faster cycle times eliminate the need for inventory of nearly all maintenance, repair, and operating items, reducing storage costs.
- Increases accountability of operating departments for purchasing decisions by transferring the purchasing power from the supply management department to the employee ordering the product.
- Reduces maverick buying. Many organizations have

"preferred" contracts in place through which significant savings are negotiated relative to "list" pricing. Industry averages suggest 20 to 25 percent premiums are paid for "off-contract" purchasing. Implementation of a comprehensive e-procurement solution empowers an organization to manage the leakage off the contracts far more easily. If just 10 percent of the buy is moved "on-contract" as a result of the control and reporting available within these solutions, an organization could reduce expenses off the top by 2 to 2.5 percent.

- Creates closer collaboration between the organization and preferred providers. With automated links directing the buy, and detailed data available regarding products purchased, received, and invoiced, organizations are better prepared to manage supplier relationships effectively.

- Increases corporate leverage. With the reporting available within the systems, organizations can determine exactly how much they are spending with various suppliers for similar commodities. This knowledge can be tremendously powerful when contracts are up for renegotiation. Organizations can prove how much was spent and can guarantee that the spend will go to the selected supplier.

90. Content is everything

Rich content drives purchasing decisions giving buyers the ability to search for products across multiple vendors and to apply complex filters to find items that meet the buyer's exact needs enabling them to make better and faster purchasing decisions. Moreover, catalogues allow sellers to differentiate their products through rich-commerce-ready product content and participate in multiple e-marketplaces without losing control of their pricing, inventory, or discounting models. To be successful, today's net market makers must deliver rich content to attract and satisfy their diverse buyer and supplier communities.

What is rich content?

Rich content is e-commerce ready product information (part number, description, supplier ratings, pricing, warranty, service info, etc.) that enables the buyers to make better and faster purchasing decisions. Some product information, such as descriptions, may be static while other information, such as price and availability, may change constantly.

91. What are the content challenges?

There are several challenges associated with content management that limit the scalability of B2B e-commerce and e-marketplaces.

• Heterogeneous data sources such as ERP systems, relational databases, flat files, web stores, etc.

- Diverse supplier terminology
- Incomplete product information
- Dynamic information such as pricing, availability, etc.
- Limited automation tools
- Poor content quality
- Lack of standards

Rich content impacts e-procurement as follows:

- Better and faster purchasing decision
- Improved sourcing capabilities
- Comparison shopping
- Ease of use ("ease of finding")
- Reduced costs
- Single content source
  Suppliers Impact
- Improved content presentation - 'differentiation'
- Ability to offer enhanced information about products
- Dramatically expand sales channel

92. Which E-Procurement Provider Is Best? How to Select a Provider.

Here is a general guide to select an e-procurement provider.

Develop a Request for Proposal: Once a short list has been developed identifying a select group of suppliers who appear to be able to meet the organizational objectives, develop a detailed request for proposal (RFP). This allows an organization to drill down and obtain specific information regarding each offering. This should include information regarding what they offer and how they offer it.

- Premise: Focus on each bidder's ability to provide a solution that achieves the desired objectives. Avoid the trap of specifying how to reach them.
- Requirements: Mandate that bidders define how the current version will meet the objectives. Be wary

of optional features, future release promises, and customization offers. There is a big difference between "we can do that," "we do do that," and "we do that now."

- Infrastructure: Obtain architecture and database diagrams, system requirements for servers and desktops; network capacity implications, remote-access solutions and methods, and number of firewall penetrations.

- Integration: Require full definition of not only what systems they will integrate, but also how they will do so, and if they have done so before.

- Suppliers: Without suppliers, an organization's e-procurement solution will be a failure. Although it may not be the most significant concern, it's a critical one. Evaluate the solution from the supplier's viewpoint. Focus on issues of cost, difficulty of integration, resource requirements to support the implementation in an ongoing fashion, and how large the supplier base is that has already been enabled for other organizations.

- Assess future direction: In an environment changing as quickly as this one, it's important to acknowledge that supply managers are buying the organization and its continued commitment to develop and enhance the solution as much as the technology. Understand the organization's source of funding, how much is invested in research and development in this particular application, plans for enhancements of the system already on the drawing board, and whether and how clients influence future enhancements.

Assess the Products: Assess the offering in total including detail on the organization that is bidding. Although the size and strength of the players in the market differ greatly, the driving factor in the final analysis is capability and functionality of the actual systems.

- Scalability and flexibility: Assess the system's ability to scale beyond the organization of today to the organization of tomorrow. Ensure that it's flexible and scalable enough to accommodate significant growth through mergers or internal development and that it's not limited by global boundaries in its ability to support the future environment.

- Back-end functionality: Process savings generated by automation of back-end connections to financial systems will account for much of the hard-dollar savings. It's critical to assess how smooth the integration will be for the financial and reporting systems of buyers and, where relevant, suppliers.

- Ease of use: Without question, if the system is difficult to use, the bulk of the population will gravitate toward a method that is easier. Success is dependent upon implementation of a user-friendly interface that encourages desired behaviors and has rapid response times. Additionally, if significant training is required, it adds time and expense to any implementation and diminishes the likelihood of success.

- Customization: This is a double-edged sword. A system that can meet operational needs with minimal customization is likely to be a much better choice than one that requires a tremendous amount of changes. The more sophisticated the organization, the less likely it will be that a vanilla implementation of any solution will address every need. Strive to find a system that can resolve critical issues through configuration during implementation, not customization of code.

- Performance: Bypass the marketing hype. Determine how many systems are operating and processing transaction activity to multiple suppliers from multiple business units. How are they working? Were the implementations relatively straightforward or extremely difficult? How similar are those implementations to what the organization's specific objectives are? Does it really do what it was promised to do by the sales team?

93. How to Analyze the Cost of E-procurement.

Here are some ways to analyze the cost: Despite the level of investment that may be required to implement any one of the alternatives under consideration, the cost of the actual software license is often a fraction of the total cost of the decision. In developing the pricing matrix and analysis, it's imperative to assess the total cost of the decision.

- License fee: Although not always the largest percentage of the cost, the license fee can be a significant investment. Have the bidders clearly define list price, discount off list price, how long the price is valid, and what is included within the base licensing fee.
- Subscription fee: In the event one chooses to outsource the acquisition of the product to an outside provider and pay for the rights to use the system on a subscription basis, there may be no upfront license fee charged, but there will be ongoing subscription fees. Be certain to obtain fixed quotes for a reasonable period, with caps on the providers' ability to increase those rates once the fixed quote has expired.
- Fee composition: Understand how the fee is computed. Run sensitivity analysis to determine under what scenarios, and at what points, additional charges will be incurred. Pricing methods vary widely from price per user, to number or value of transactions processed, to site licenses, and many combinations thereof. As a

result, it's often difficult to complete a fair comparison of solutions using different pricing mechanisms.

- Authorized users: Be careful to clearly define what parts of the organization are covered under the agreement. Does it include subsidiaries, parent affiliates, and even subcontractors or other partner organizations? What happens if the organization buys another organization? What happens if it sells part of the existing organization?
- Annual support and maintenance fees: Typically, maintenance is priced on a percentage of prices paid for the license or service. Clearly define the percentage, under what circumstances that percentage may rise and by how much, and on what basis the percentage is calculated for current and future acquisitions.
- Costs of upgrades: An organization's best leverage is during the initial procurement decision. Now is the time to negotiate specific pricing for future upgrades. If a fixed quote is unobtainable, at minimum, negotiate a committed discount off of list price.
- Consulting costs for implementation: Clearly scope out the expected deliverable for a comprehensive installation and implementation of the solution into the environment. Be wary of vague estimates based on general project plans. Provide the bidders sufficient information regarding the current and future proposed environment so that they will be able to develop organization-specific estimates. Negotiate the hourly rates as well as incentive arrangements and expenses.
- Internal costs: Include all relevant costs, such as time for internal resources to implement and integrate the system initially, and manage and administer the system going forward. Calculate the hard-dollar costs

to upgrade the internal network, desktop, and server hardware as necessary to support the new system.

- Other third-party costs: Do not forget to compute the costs that will be incurred if the system needs to integrate to other third-party systems, and what fees are incurred by those third-party providers to support the development of system-specific feeds or bridges.

94. How to Conduct an E-procurement Reality Test.

All too often, the differences between what suppliers can demonstrate and what the system is capable of doing are significant. At times, it's as simple as a misunderstanding relative to the intent of the question asked in the RFP. Nearly every system can do things with sufficient customization. If it does as a matter of course or as part of the base package is of concern to the evaluators.

- Hold a scripted demonstration: Require each bidder to demonstrate specific functionality that meets the business requirements defined early in the process. Have them demonstrate the steps that it takes to "make" certain processes happen. Focus on functions and activities that will be performed by end users, power users, and system administration staff to get a comprehensive picture of how intuitive the system is to use.
- Check references: Become familiar with the supplier's clients. Ask what they implemented and why. Understand what other systems were evaluated and why they were not selected. Ask the tough questions about what went wrong, the pitfalls in the implementation process, and whether they got what they were promised, or minimally what they expected.

- Schedule customer visits: Get a firsthand look at how live end users navigate throughout the system. See how programmers and project managers feel about the system. Ask detailed questions about the pains of implementation, the ease of upgrade installation, and migration and user acceptance.

The above checklist items and plan will help in the right selection.

95. Expect the Best from Your People. They Can Be the Best.

Set the standards of performance for yourself and your people high. Expectation setting is critical to success. Reward outstanding performance not average. Encourage purchasing professionals to become experts in a market, industry or supplier group. Most of all encourage them to know your business, the cost drivers and the end customer needs and strive to exceed them.

96. Sometimes You Must Punt on Third Down. Punt.

Do Not expect every market analysis or supplier selection to go smoothly. At times market conditions are not buyer favorable and no amount of planning, negotiations or cooperation will yield any mutually beneficial results.

Cut your losses and revisit the market at a more favorable time.

97. Sometimes Your Worst Suppliers Are Your Own Internal Divisions

Once when I was in the paper industry we were in desperate need of base paper stock to convert into napkins because out own machines had extensive downtime. Our "sister" plant on the west coast came to our rescue and shipped us base paper rolls to meet the need. We were initially glad to get some help. We soon discovered that they had loaded the rolls in boxcars and extensively damaged them. We had to cut off the damaged paper. The boxcars were also loaded in a haphazard manner and took very long periods to unload. On top of these issues they must have seen this as an opportunity to ship all their old off quality rolls. The quality was terrible. The rolls took twice as long to convert into napkins. Needless to say we never asked for their help again. All too often a company's own internal divisions do not treat their internal customers with any degree of respect. The standards must be at least the same if not better than for your final customer. Purchasing should lead the setting of these standards.

98. Preaching to the Choir. Do not.

Most purchasing folks want to do the right thing and be more strategic rather than tactical. The antiquated processes and systems drag them down and inhibit any initiative. Certainty keeping their morale high during a transformation process is essential. Overkill will however produce skepticism and distrust. Let them learn and make mistakes that they can learn even more from. Make sure they network with each other and share lessons learned. You need to make them grizzled veterans quickly.

99. Keep Selling the Transformation or Reengineering. Sell. Sell. Sell.

Your need to spend at least 30-40% of your time getting the word out to folks on your strategy, messages and plans. You cannot over communicate especially about something as radical as transforming purchasing. It requires above all discipline and a constant reminder to make sure folks understand why you are doing certain steps, programs and strategies. Keep the metrics right in front of them and enlist your suppliers to help your spread the message.

100. Persevere.

No matter how rough the process gets losing your temper or wavering from your goals will not help your cause. People can detect the indomitable spirit. You need to make sure that they understand that this is not just another program that will fade away.

Keep telling yourself that you will prevail and eventually you will!

General References:

Institute for Supply Management
Supply Management Institute
Gartner Group Articles
Various Internet Articles
Dr. Tom's Purchasing Experiences and Articles

Visit the website www.commonsensepurchasing.com for more common sense purchasing information.

Index

Printed by Amazon Italia Logistica S.r.l.
Torrazza Piemonte (TO), Italy

10925847R00058